STRUCTURES

BRIDGES

Andrew Dunn

Wayland

Titles in the series

Bridges
Dams
Skyscrapers
Tunnels

Words that appear in the
glossary are printed in **bold**
the first time they appear
in the text.

Editor: Kathryn Smith

Series designer: Joyce Chester

First published in 1993

by Wayland (Publishers) Ltd

61 Western Road, Hove

East Sussex BN3 1JD, England

British Library Cataloguing in Publication Data

Dunn, Andrew

Bridges. -(Structures Series)

I. Title II. Series

624

ISBN 0 7502 0495 8

Typeset by Key Origination, Eastbourne, Sussex

Printed by G. Canale & C.S.p.A., Turin

Contents

*Calstock Viaduct
over the River
Tamar in south
Devon, England.*

1 What are bridges for?

Bridges, big and small, make our lives easier. They take us over rivers, deep gorges and obstacles that would otherwise make a long **detour** necessary. They make travelling quicker by making journeys shorter. Indeed, without bridges some journeys would not be possible at all. Other bridges across wide rivers have replaced ferry services.

Crossing this river without getting wet could pose problems. A long detour may be necessary, before you can get to the other side. A bridge would make life easier.

In tropical parts of the world, people learned to use vines and creepers to make rope bridges. A bundle of ropes was stretched over a river for people to walk on, with two other ropes for handrails. This rope bridge is spectacularly overgrown with tree roots and creepers.

Crossings which used to take hours by ferry now take only minutes. Bridges carry footpaths, roads, railways and waterways over valleys, rivers and seas, and over other roads, railways and waterways. They are structures which are important to all of us, and they can be both beautiful and impressive.

BRIDGES IN HISTORY

The first bridges were simply trees which had fallen across streams. Primitive people probably looked at these and put tree trunks across streams at convenient places to make their own bridges. Soon blocks of stone – stepping stones – were placed in rivers so that people could step

This three-arched bridge was built in the second century BC in Turkey. No cement was used to build the arches. Pressure alone keeps the stones together.

from one to another to get across. Stepping-stones led to the first structures that we would reconize as bridges; so-called clapper bridges, made of flat slabs of stone placed across stepping-stones. Clapper bridges can still be seen today.

A big advance in bridge-building came with the arch bridge. An arch can **span** a wider gap than a simple beam and is much stronger. Its strength does not come from the material it is made of, but from its shape. The arch structure was used by the Chinese, Babylonians, Greeks and Romans. But the oldest bridge we know of, believed by historians to have been an arch, was built over the River Nile in ancient Egypt about 4,650 years ago. The oldest surviving single-arch bridge is one built over the River Meles in Turkey about 2,840 years ago. The fact that it still exists today shows what a good **design** the arch is.

Bridge-builders have always learned from the skills and experience of those who built bridges before them. The ancient Romans brought the arch to Europe from Asia, and began building out of stone instead of wood. In the Middle Ages, as trade grew and people travelled more, many bridges were built. Some had chapels, rest houses for travellers, or even prisons on them. Bridges in towns often had defences at one end to stop invaders.

> **The famous London Bridge, begun in 1176, had nineteen pointed arches. It had a drawbridge section which could be raised to allow big ships underneath, and gates at either end to defend the city. The structure lasted for over 600 years.**

The most recent type of bridge is the suspension bridge, a modern version of the rope bridge. Suspension bridges are now the longest and most spectacular bridges there are.

Why do different bridges have the shapes they do? Why do they not fall down under the strain of heavy weights? The answers lie in many years of experience, the intelligent use of the laws of nature, and magnificent **engineering** skills.

MAKE A SUSPENSION BRIDGE

What you need:
Two friends; two chairs; two lengths of rope; string; a plank of wood and some books.
What you do:
Place the chairs facing back to back about a metre apart. Lay the ropes side by side over them, and ask your friends to hold the ends on the ground. Cut the string into several pieces the same length (about 50 cm). Tie them to the ropes to form hanging loops, and use them to support the plank.
Use the books as weights on the bridge. How much will it hold? What happens if your friends do not hold the ropes tightly enough? Can you see why firm anchorages are so important in bridge building?

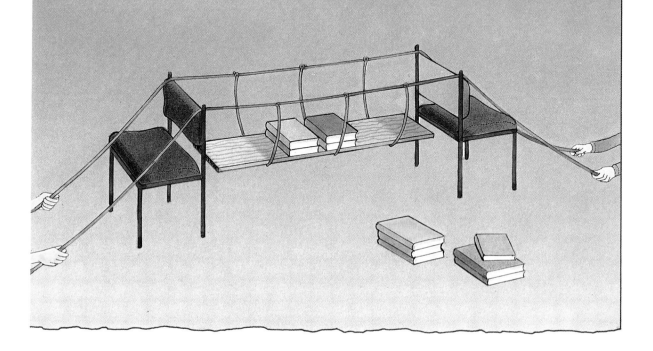

2 The technology of bridges

BELOW
*This simple
beam bridge in
Ontario, Canada,
has the longest
single wooden
span (70 m) in
the world.*

*Diagram to show
the forces at
work on a beam
bridge.*

DIFFERENT TYPES OF BRIDGE

There are four main types of bridge: beam bridges, cantilevers, arch and suspension bridges.
Beam bridges are the simplest and most common kind of bridge. A plank over a stream is a simple example. The weight of the beam pushes straight down, and is supported by the land or **piers** on either side. The beam itself must be very strong, or it will bend under the weight of traffic. Beams can be made stronger by using **trusses** or **girders** – long narrow rods – often in triangular patterns. Even so, the distance between supports, the span,

cannot be very long. One way of making beam bridges longer is to build several supporting piers underneath them. One variation on the simple beam is the *box-girder bridge*, like Robert Stephenson's Britannia Railway Bridge over the Menai Strait in Wales. Finished in 1850, it consisted of strong hollow boxes made of iron plates, through which trains ran. Another variation is the *cable-stayed bridge*. This has cables stretched from towers high above supporting piers to the beam. This strengthens the bridge and holds it steady.

Arches have great natural strength. They do not press straight downwards as beams do. Instead, all the weight of the bridge is evenly spread around the arch to its ends, which are anchored firmly in the ground, pressing against the **foundations**, called **abutments**.

BELOW Although the arch of this bridge is tiny in comparison to the arches in the picture above, they have been built using the same principles.

An arch bridge is usually built around a temporary frame, called falsework. When it is complete, it holds itself up and the falsework is removed.

Many arch bridges used to be built of stone; blocks were placed around the falsework. When the final wedge-shaped stone at the top (the keystone) was inserted, the arch would stay up without any **cement** because all the blocks pushed on each other.

The Romans built many multi-arch bridges, where each arch transfers the weight to its neighbour until it reaches the bank. As well as road bridges, the Romans built **aqueducts**, to carry water into their towns. Many still exist today. In the last century, engineers building the railways copied the Roman designs to build **viaducts** across valleys.

LEFT This spectacular aqueduct, the Pont du Gard, in France, was built by the Romans.

BELOW Australia's Sydney Harbour Bridge spans 503 m, carrying four railway lines, eight road lanes, one cycle lane and a footpath.

Diagram to show forces at work on an arch bridge.

With the development of modern materials such as steel and **concrete**, engineers found they could build bigger arches. This meant that they could build bridges over deep, wide rivers used by big ships. Most arch bridges have a road or railway running over the top. But one famous arch bridge – Australia's Sydney Harbour Bridge, opened in 1932 – has its **decking** hung below. It spans 503 m, and carries four railways, eight road lanes, a cycle lane and a footpath.

The bridge was built without false-work, so that the harbour could stay open. Two steel arches were built out from each bank, piece by piece, and were held up by cables anchored to the ground behind the abutments.

A *cantilever bridge* depends on balance, and can span long distances. Each section has a central pillar or pier, with a beam jutting out from either side. It looks like a letter 'T', or someone with their arms spread out sideways. One arm is anchored firmly to the bank, pulling on it, and it balances the other arm (the cantilever).

Often the arms are strengthened by struts from the central pillar. Usually the arms of the two sections do not meet, but are joined by a span suspended high above the water, allowing ships to pass below.

The famous Forth Railway Bridge near Edinburgh, Scotland, is surely the world's most impressive cantilever bridge. It has three sections, so the middle section is not attached to either bank. One of the first bridges to be made of steel (59,000 tonnes of it), and 2,529 m long, it has carried trains for over a century. It is a great engineering feat. It takes a team of 29 painters three years to paint the entire bridge, in order to stop it rusting. When they have finished, they have to start all over again!

Suspension bridges can span much wider distances than any other kind of bridge, and have no supports below to get in the way of river traffic. The decking hangs from two huge cables which rest on a tower at each end. The cables are firmly attached to the ground beyond each of the towers. The huge weight of the bridge is carried partly by the towers.

BELOW
The Forth Railway Bridge is surely the world's most impressive cantilever bridge. It was one of the first bridges to be made of steel.

Diagram to show the forces at work on a Cantilever bridge.

Diagram to show the forces at work on a suspension bridge.

The Golden Gate suspension bridge, California, USA, spans 1280 m across the entrance to San Francisco Harbour.

Most is carried by cables, which transfer weight to the **anchorages.**

The first modern suspension bridges were built early in the nineteenth century, using iron chains as cables. Chains were soon replaced by twisted bundles of wires. Now suspension bridges are made of concrete and **steel**, making them light, slim and graceful but extremely strong. Some of the most spectacular include the Verrazano Narrows Bridge in New York, Turkey's Bosporos bridges, joining Europe to Asia, the famous Golden Gate Bridge over San Francisco Bay, and the longest single-span bridge in the world, the Humber Bridge in England.

BRIDGING THE GAP

What you need:

Some stiff paper or card; two piles of books; pebbles or coins (for weights) in a plastic tub; three toilet paper tubes; scissors; sticky tape.

What you do:

Place the two piles of books about 50 cm apart. Try different ways of bridging the gap between them, and see how much weight you can place on each before it collapses.

Try: 1. a flat strip of card.

2. a piece of card folded many times lengthways, with a flat strip on top.

3. a flat strip of card with the cardboard tube 'piers' underneath.

4. a strip of card bent into an arch shape, with a flat strip on top.

Try adding more books on top of the bridge's ends to hold down the card. Can you think of other shapes to try? How about a tube?

Why are some shapes stronger than others? Which are strongest?

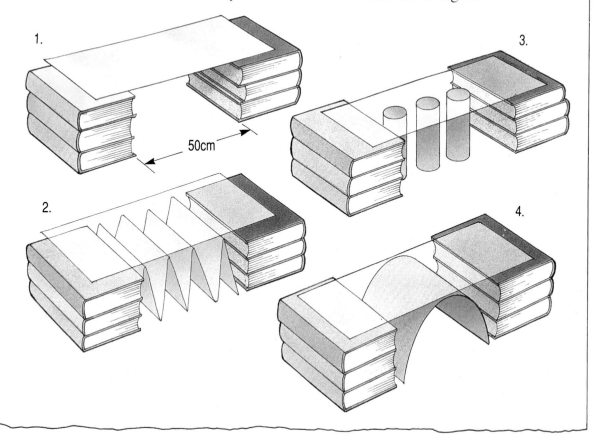

1.

50cm

2.

3.

4.

3 How a bridge is built: bridging the Humber

Before building any bridge, designers have to decide which type is most suitable. The Humber Estuary, on England's east coast, is wide and busy with shipping. So a very ambitious suspension bridge was chosen.

The foundations of a bridge are very important. On the north side of the Humber there is firm chalk. But on the south bank there is soft clay.

So the south tower was built in the river itself, with the cables anchored on the bank. First, a model of the bridge was tested in a wind tunnel to check that the bridge would survive gales. Then the two 155 m high towers were built. Each has two hollow concrete legs, with lifts inside them. The north tower went up quickly, but building the south tower on the clay proved much more difficult and very slow.

By 1992 the Humber Bridge was beginning to rust from the inside. The steel decking needed protection from the moist air which causes rust. Engineers decided to dry the air, using a kind of giant hair-dryer and a chemical that absorbs moisture.

It was built using **caissons** – round concrete tubes sunk into the river-bed – so that the water could be carefully pumped out.

The massive concrete anchorages were built at the same time. To make sure the anchorage on the soft south bank can take the strain, it weighs 300,000 tonnes!

Then the two immense main cables were spun. A device like a bicycle wheel, carrying thin steel wire, travelled back and forth above the water. 15,000 wires were spun and bound together to make each cable –

71,000 km of wire altogether, weighing 11,000 tonnes. Then very strong hangers were attached to support the road deck.

The deck was made in 124 sections. Each 140-tonne steel box was floated out and hoisted into position by cranes. Then they were welded together. The bridge opened in 1981, ten years after planning began.

The spinning of the main cables began in September 1977 and was finished in July 1979. Each cable is made up of 14,949 wires which are divided into 37 strands. Here, workmen lay each strand into place at the cap of the tower.

COMPRESSION AND TENSION: PUSHING AND PULLING

What stops a bridge from collapsing? How can a bridge support the huge weight of traffic which drives over it daily? The weight of a bridge and its traffic puts immense forces on the structure and its supports. The main ones are pushing forces – compression – and pulling, called tension.

In an arch bridge, each part of the arch pushes on the next part. The whole weight of the bridge pushes into the abutments at either end, which must be very strong. An arch is under compression.

In a suspension bridge, the towers are pushed down by their sheer weight. They are under compression. At the same time the cables pull on their anchorages, so they are under tension. These are the forces which are at work to keep the bridge standing. Engineers have to calculate the forces carefully, to make sure the cables, beams, girders and so on are strong enough for the job. They must also choose the right materials.

TENSION AND COMPRESSION

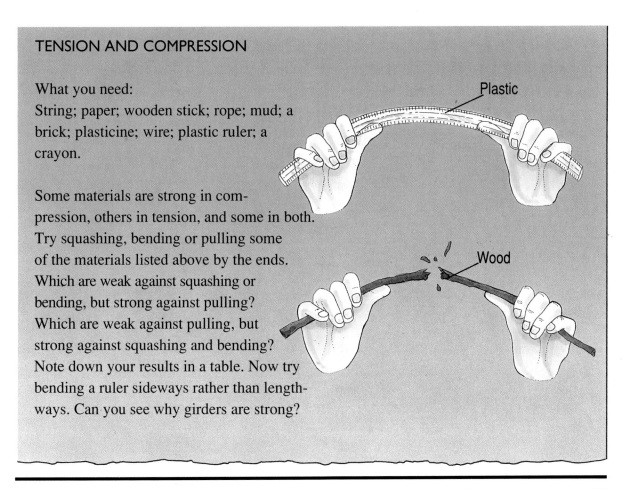

What you need:
String; paper; wooden stick; rope; mud; a brick; plasticine; wire; plastic ruler; a crayon.

Some materials are strong in compression, others in tension, and some in both. Try squashing, bending or pulling some of the materials listed above by the ends. Which are weak against squashing or bending, but strong against pulling? Which are weak against pulling, but strong against squashing and bending? Note down your results in a table. Now try bending a ruler sideways rather than lengthways. Can you see why girders are strong?

Can you see the steel wires sticking out of the concrete of this bridge? Combining concrete with steel makes a superb material. Reinforced concrete has steel wires inside it. Stretching the wires before the concrete dries makes prestressed concrete, which is extremely strong.

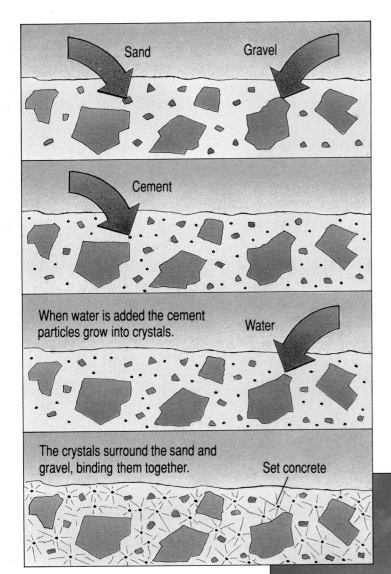

How concrete is made

CHOOSING THE RIGHT MATERIALS

At first, bridges were built of wood, stone or iron. Steel, stronger and lighter than iron, became available in the mid-nineteenth century. It is extremely strong in tension.

Concrete was developed soon after steel. It is made of sand and gravel, held together with a glue of cement and water. It can be poured into moulds to make beams, columns, or almost any shape. It is very strong in compression.

Other new materials may soon be used. **Carbon fibres**, for instance, are stronger and lighter than steel wires. Engineers are always looking for new, stronger materials and different uses for them.

This railway bridge over a valley in west Germany is constructed almost entirely of reinforced concrete.

The benefits of bridges

Bridges have been important throughout history. As primitive peoples began to farm, and develop civilizations, they also started trading with each other. Much trade was done by sea, but long overland trade routes also developed, some-times across whole continents. Bridges were often needed on trade routes to overcome obstacles.

Bridges have always been important in war, too. Armies often try to take possession of bridges in wartime because an army that controls a

Temporary Bailey Bridges are used by armies, especially in wartime. Here, a section of a Bailey bridge is being used as a ferry to cross a river.

country's bridges usually controls that country's supplies. Modern armies use temporary bridges called 'Bailey' bridges, that can be carried on the back of a lorry and thrown across a river. Once the troops are across, the bridge can be pulled up quickly to prevent an enemy crossing.

But bridges are mostly used to help people keep in touch with one another. Before bridges such as the Sydney Harbour Bridge, the Golden Gate Bridge or the Humber Bridge were built, people had to go far upstream to cross, or take a slow ferry. With the development of railways in the nineteenth

The arrival of the motorway in the twentieth century has meant that many more road bridges have been built, such as the famous Europa Brucke of the Brenner Autobahn in Austria.

century, and motorways in the twentieth century, many new bridges were built. These included large road and railway bridges, and many small bridges, built to help people and animals cross roads and railway lines safely.

Bridges can also help the **environment**, and save money. Shorter journeys use less fuel, energy and time. That means less **pollution**, lower costs – and fewer tired drivers! On the other hand big new bridges encourage extra traffic, and they cost a great deal of money to build. Every driver who crosses the Humber Bridge or the Golden Gate Bridge pays a **toll**.

Many bridges enrich the scenery. What would San Francisco be like without its spectacular Golden Gate Bridge? Or London without its Tower Bridge? New York's Verrazano Narrows Bridge is one of the most elegant structures in the world.

And when people think of Sydney, most picture in their minds its famous Harbour Bridge, with the stunning Opera House close by.

However, it will be many years before the huge cost has been paid off. Even then, bridges are expensive to keep in good repair. So when a new bridge is suggested, planners have to decide whether the benefits it will bring are worth the price.

Like any big structure, building a bridge involves a lot of disruption, and new roads or railways usually have to be built to reach it. But a well-designed bridge is beautiful in itself.

A well-designed bridge can enrich the scenery. Here, the magnificent aqueduct the Ponte del Torri graces the hills near San Pieto in Italy.

THE FAR SIDE

Imagine that you are alive over 1000 years ago. You live in a small, isolated farming village on the banks of a deep, wide river. Crossing the river has always been difficult, and few people from the village have ever been over to the other side. A new bridge is built across the river.
Write a short story describing your first journey across the bridge. How does the arrival of the bridge change your life, and the lives of the other villagers?

5 Problems and disasters

The Tay Bridge over the Firth of Tay near Dundee in Scotland was finished in 1878. On the night of 28 December 1897 a section of the bridge collapsed, revealing serious faults in the design.

Bridges, like dams and sky-scrapers, have to withstand the powerful forces of nature, as well as their own weight and the loads they carry. Over the centuries, engineers have learned from experience how to build the right kind of bridge for the job, safely and strongly. Yet mistakes still happen, and bridges do collapse sometimes. Two famous bridge disasters led to major changes in the way bridges are built. Both were caused by the wind.

The Tay Bridge, finished in 1878, was a beam bridge made of trusses of iron girders standing on many iron

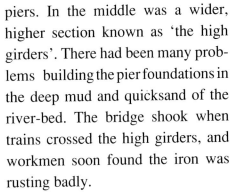

piers. In the middle was a wider, higher section known as 'the high girders'. There had been many problems building the pier foundations in the deep mud and quicksand of the river-bed. The bridge shook when trains crossed the high girders, and workmen soon found the iron was rusting badly.

Sunday 28 December, 1879 was a wild, windy night. As the evening train passed on to the bridge, a signal-man heard a loud drumming noise. Then there was a shower of sparks and a terrific groaning noise of wrenching metal. In the howling wind, the railwayman crawled on to the bridge. Where the high girders had been he found nothing but a gaping hole. Thirteen spans had collapsed into the black river, taking the train and seventy-five people with it. No one survived.

The bridge had been badly built. Its designer also admitted that he had not taken wind into account. His design for another bridge, which had already begun construction, was scrapped. The new engineers decided

to use steel, and allowed for strong winds in their plans. The result was the bridge which still stands there today.

In 1940, a big suspension bridge was opened over Tacoma Narrows in Washington State, USA. Four months later, when a fairly strong wind blew up, the narrow flexible deck started to buck up and down wildly. Then it began to twist as well. Fortunately this time there was enough warning to close the bridge, and the bridge was even filmed tearing itself to bits. It turned out that the bridge reacted to the wind in a way which had been little understood before. It vibrated in sympathy to its buffeting by the wind, rather like a guitar string does when it is plucked.

In fact, the idea of bridges acting like guitar strings was not new. Many centuries ago it was realized that columns of troops marching in step across a bridge could set up vibrations that might shake a bridge enough to destroy it. Even today, soldiers stop marching when they cross a bridge.

Bridges have to be able to withstand other forces too. Rivers running below can wash piers away. In earthquake areas, the foundations must be very strong, and the bridge itself must be shake-proof.

When a strong earthquake hit San Francisco in 1989, there were surprisingly few casualties – but several people were killed by collapsing bridge sections of a freeway.

The Tacoma Narrows Bridge disaster took place in 1940, Washington State, USA. This disastrous failure led to a complete change in suspension bridge deck design. Now the deck of a suspension bridge is shaped so that air flows around it, but it remains stiff at the same time.

6

The interesting and the unusual

The city of London's famous Tower Bridge is worked by hydraulic machinery.

Bridges can solve problems in some clever ways.

MOVING BRIDGES

Most bridges are designed to be firm and solid, whatever the weather. But some are meant to move. High bridges over rivers and canals can be very expensive, and are not always possible. The answer is to build a low bridge which can move to let big ships pass underneath.

Tower Bridge, opened in 1894, is London's most famous bridge.

A lifting bridge spans the St Lawrence River at Montreal in Canada. The bridge is not hinged, but cables in towers at each end lift the whole span upwards out of the way.

Swing bridges do not move up and down, but turn on a pivot so that ships can pass by the side. Then they swing back across the waterway to join up the road on either side.

The transporter bridge is another way round the problem. The Rendsberg Bridge over the Kiel Canal in Germany is a high-level railway bridge, but the road runs at ground level. Cars drive into a cage hanging from the girders above, which is then winched across the river to the road on the other side.

STRANGE BRIDGES

In places where the banks or river-bed are too soft to support any foundations, a floating pontoon bridge might be used. It can be made from hollow concrete blocks which float on the water. They are anchored to the river-bed by cables. A road or railway can be placed on top.

It is also the world's best-known moving bridge. The road span is in two sections, called bascules, each hinged at one end. They can be lifted up like a drawbridge to let ships through. Even though each bascule weighs 1,120 tonnes, the **hydraulic** machinery can raise them in four minutes.

This pontoon bridge in Cape, South Africa, is used like a ferry service to transport people and goods between the river banks.

Some bridges are unique – the only ones of their kind in the world. The longest bridge in the world is a **causeway** in Louisiana, USA, which crosses Lake Pontchartrain. It is over 38 km long and built of hundreds of concrete spans. It is so long that from the middle, no land can be seen. The New Orleans Mardi Gras Marathon race is run over it.

The Crawford Street Bridge in Providence, Rhode Island, USA, is 350 m wide – wider than most bridges are long!

The USA's Chesapeake Bay Bridge, is a combination bridge, 28 km long. It includes sections of beam bridges, cantilever, and suspension bridges – and two tunnels! Another combination bridge is the Great Seto.

This bridge between Honshu and Shikoku islands in Japan, has six suspension spans linked by viaducts in its 12.8 km length. It carries a roadway above a railway. Crossing used to take an hour by ferry; now it takes ten minutes by car.

One bridge became the largest antique ever sold. In March 1968, London Bridge was sold for just over £1,000,000 to an American oil company, which took all 10,000 tonnes of it across to the USA and rebuilt it in a desert in Arizona.

Bridge builders nearly always find answers to difficult problems. The River Tamar in Tasmania, Australia, has hard rock on one side, but soft clay on the other. So a half-suspension, half-cabled-stayed

This spectacular view shows the Seto Ohashi Bridge from Mount Washu in Japan. The bridge links the Honshu and Shikoku islands.

The Akashi-Kaikyo Bridge in Japan was begun in 1988, and is due to be completed in 1998. Its main suspension span will be 1990 m long, and its towers 297 m high. But even this will not be the longest bridge for long. There are plans to build a bridge linking Italy and Sicily across the Messina Strait, pictured here.

bridge, nicknamed 'Batman', was designed, which supports nearly all the weight from the rocky side.

Engineers and designers will never cease trying new materials and designs, and to build bridges that are bigger, better and safer than any before.

Next time you go on a long journey by car, bus or train, look at the bridges you pass under or over. Make a sketch of each one. What shape are they? Are they beam bridges, cantilevers, arches or suspension bridges? What are they made of? Try to think why they were built the way they were.

Glossary

Abutments Parts of the structures designed to take the weight or force of the parts next to them. In an arch bridge, the abutments take the whole weight, so they must be strong and solid.

Anchorages The places where the cables are fixed. The cable ends are tied to strong steel bars buried in enormous concrete structures, which hold them so firmly, they cannot be pulled out.

Aqueducts Bridges built to carry flowing water from one place to another.

Caissons Round concrete tubes sunk into a river-bed until they reach solid ground. Mud and water are pumped out, and the bottom sealed with concrete. The caissons then become the foundations for the bridge's piers or towers.

Carbon fibres Strings or threads of carbon, the element from which charcoal, diamonds and pencil-leads are made. In carbon fibres the carbon is arranged in a special way to make it very strong.

Causeway A raised path or road crossing a marsh or shallow water.

Cement A glue for sticking bricks or stones together. Made from ground-up limestone and clay with water, it sets hard as it dries.

Concrete A mixture of cement and gravel, which is used in building.

Decking The part of the bridge which carries the road, railway or path.

Design A shape that has been planned or intended. A designer is someone who plans the shape and look of something.

Detour A long, winding way from place to place instead of the shortest way.

Engineering The art of building complicated structures or machines. [Civil engineers build roads, bridges and buildings. There are also mechanical, electronic, chemical, and many other kinds of engineering.]

Environment Everything around us (and all living things) – the air we breathe, the land we live on, the water we drink, and so on.

Foundation The solid base on which a bridge (or any structure) stands.

Girders Strong metal beams used for support. Viewed end-on, they often have an 'I' shape, which stops them bending.

Hydraulic Operated by fluids, such as gas or oil, under high pressure. Hydraulic machines are very powerful.

Piers Pillars built below bridges for support.

Pollution Waste gases (such as exhaust fumes), liquids and solids which poison our surroundings (the environment), and harm or even kill plants and animals.

Pre-stressed Concrete in which wires, stretched before the concrete dried, try to pull back to their original length. They try to make the beam shorter, stressing it and making it very strong.

Reinforced Made even stronger.

Span To bridge over a gap. A span is the part of a bridge between two supports.

Steel A very strong metal made from iron hardened by the addition of a little carbon.

Toll A charge paid to a bridge-keeper for crossing the bridge.

Trusses Frameworks of beams or girders, used for extra support.

Viaducts A long bridge that carries a road or a railway over a valley.

Further reading

Bridges by Kate Petty & Terry Cash (A&C Black, 1990)

Bridges by Graham Rickard (Wayland, 1986)

Building Technology by Mark Lambert (Wayland, 1991)

How We Build Bridges by Neil Ardley (Macmillan, 1989)

Structures by Malcolm Dixon (Wayland, 1990)

PICTURE ACKNOWLEDGEMENTS

Aspect 4 (A. Greeman), 26, 28; B. Coleman 3, 5 (A. Compost), 6 (P. Terry), 9 (W. Lankinen), 10 top (H. Kranawetter), bottom (J. Fryer), 13 (S. Alden), 15 (A. Purcell), 19 (T. Buckholz), 21 (N. Rosing); Eye Ubiquitous cover; Mary Evans 7, 23; J. Holmes 27; David Lee 16; Topham 20, 24; Tony Stone 11 (L. Meier), 22 (J. Cornish); Zefa 12 (Weir), 18 (Steichan), 25, 28. Artwork by Steve Wheele on pages 8, 14, 17, 19. Artwork by Nick Hawken on pages 9, 11, 12, 13.

Index